Vintage Political

Illustrations

Ephemera

Jaci Abraham

THE SENATE

PROGRESSIVE LEGISLATION
TARIFF REVISION
R.R. RATE BILL

SHIP BUILDERS' TRUST

JEFFERSON!
JEFFERSONISM!!
JEFFERSONIAN
SIMPLICITY!!!

MARS

PEACE
WAR

CHINA
KOREA
JAPAN

THE FOREIGNER PAYS THE TAX
PRESIDENTIAL HOPES
BUSINESS
REVIVAL

PANAMA CANAL ROUTE
CENTRAL AMERICA

THE DOUMA
RUSSIA

LAWSON
OUTCAST
REJECTED

SOCIETY'S DIVORCE
RECORD

—DIVORCED YESTERDAY—

ROCKSLEY FROM ROCKSLEY
VAN SWELL " VAN SWELL
TINIT " WRIGHTINIT

—MARRIED TO-DAY—

ROCKSLEY TO VAN SWELL
AN SWELL " WRIGHT
TINIT " ROCKSLEY

PRUSSIA

PEACE

"REDUCTION IN WAGES"
DUE TO THE GREAT LAW
OF SUPPLY AND DEMAND
EXPLANATION BY
REPUBLICAN PARTY
UNDER
REPUBLICAN ADMINISTRATION

BRYAN
IN HIS
GREAT PLAY
CONSERVATISM
IN HIS ROARING FARCE
FREE SILVER
JONES

HEE HAW
DEMOCRATIC PARTY
STANDPATTER
INSURGENTS
G.O.P.

COMMON SENSE TOBACCO

TO THE HAGUE
PLAN OF ARBITRATION SUBMITTED BY THE UNITED STATES

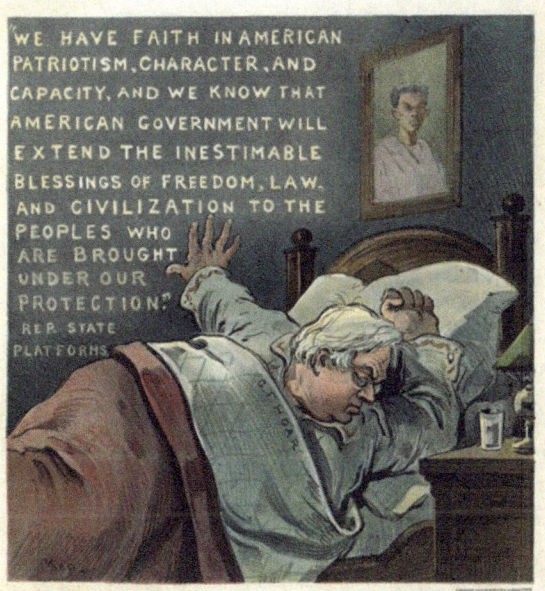

ROTTEN FINANCE

CONFIDENCE

HUMPTY DUMPTY SAT ON A WALL,
HUMPTY DUMPTY HAD A GREAT FALL,
ALL THE STREET'S HORSES AND ALL THE STREET'S MEN
CAN'T PUT HUMPTY BACK AGAIN.

THE PRESIDENCY

1912

UNITED STATES BULLETIN BOARD

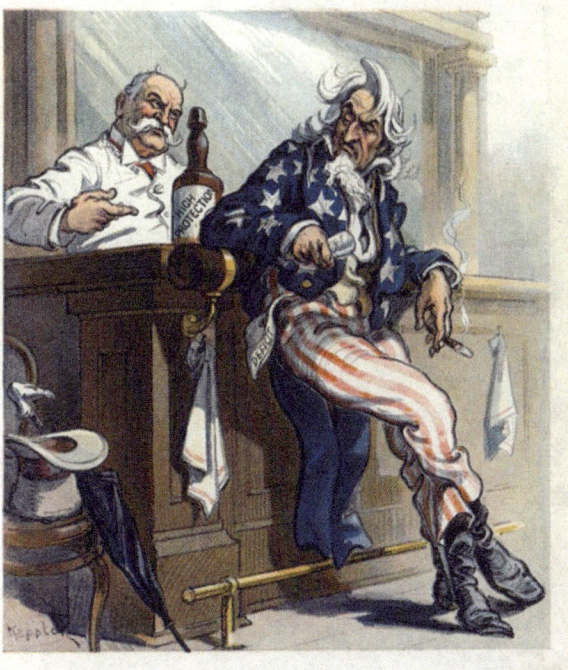

COAL STRIKES

INDUSTRY

DINGLEY TARIFF

SECTION

22

AMENDMENT TO SECTION 22 OF THE TARIFF ACT IMPOSING DISCRIMINATING DUTIES ON GOODS SHIPPED THROUGH CANADA TO THE UNITED STATES

Keppler

CASHIER   VICE-PRES   PRESIDENT

COLLATERAL

GRAND BENEFIT IN BEHALF OF STRIKING COALMINERS OF PENNSYLVANIA

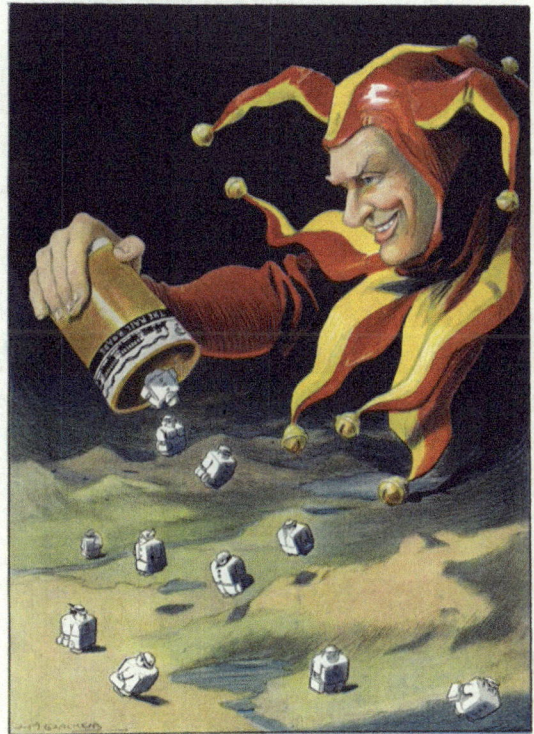

Made in the USA
Las Vegas, NV
21 April 2025

21222169R00044